T0083155

WILLIAM WALTON

arr. Robert Gower

ORB AND SCEPTRE

Coronation March, 1953

MUSIC DEPARTMENT

OXFORD
UNIVERSITY PRESS

Orb and Sceptre

(Coronation March, 1953)

WILLIAM WALTON
arr. Robert Gower

* Passages in square brackets may be played on a solo reed.

© Oxford University Press 1953 and 1996

Printed in Great Britain

OXFORD UNIVERSITY PRESS, MUSIC DEPARTMENT, GREAT CLARENDON STREET, OXFORD OX2 6DP

The Moral Rights of the Composer have been asserted. Photocopying this copyright material is ILLEGAL.

f
f marcato
pomposo
marcato
ff

p
mp
mf
sempre cresc.
ff brillante

to Coda

f marcato
mf sempre dim.
Molto espressivo
e sostenuto
Gt.
p
Sw.
Gt. to Ped. off

maestoso
Gt.
f
Gt.
+ Gt. to Ped.

Come prima
D.S. al poi al Coda
ff
ff
[f
CODA
5
5
[ ]
[ ]

accel.
mf cresc.
Allegro
ff
rit.

Largamente
ff molto legato
subito vivace

Full organ
fff